Talk It Out

T0021642

To get the complete **Idioms for Inclusivity** experience, this book can be purchased alongside four others as a set, *Idioms for Inclusivity: Fostering Belonging with Language*, **978-1-032-28635-8**.

Informed by sociolinguistic research, yet written accessibly, *Talk It Out* challenges readers to investigate disagreeing with someone as it relates to both language-use and inclusivity.

This engaging and delightfully illustrated book invites students to engage with concepts such as:

- the cultural meaning of the idiom "talk it out"

- Facework and Politeness Theory, two frameworks that linguists use to research and understand disagreements

- why it can be so hard to like someone who disagrees with you

- why the expectation to "talk it out" could make someone feel excluded

- how understanding the way language works can help us learn to be more inclusive

Featuring practical inclusivity tips related to integrating learning into daily conversations, this enriching curriculum supplement can be used in a Language Arts setting to learn about figurative language; in a Social Studies setting to discuss diversity, equity, inclusion, and belonging; or as an introduction to linguistics for students aged 7–14.

Samantha Beaver is a workplace communications analyst and linguist. She has been involved in language research and teaching/training since 2013. She is currently CEO and Founder of Memra Language Services.

Discover the other books in the *Idioms for Inclusivity: Fostering Belonging with Language* **set**
Available from Routledge (www.routledge.com)

Keep Your Word: Discussing Promises
Written by Samantha Beaver
Illustrated by Melissa Lee Johnson

Speak for Yourself: Discussing Assumptions
Written by Samantha Beaver
Illustrated by Melissa Lee Johnson

Use Your Voice: Discussing Identity
Written by Samantha Beaver
Illustrated by Melissa Lee Johnson

Use Your Words: Discussing Articulation
Written by Samantha Beaver
Illustrated by Melissa Lee Johnson

TALK IT OUT

DISCUSSING DISAGREEMENT

SAMANTHA BEAVER

ILLUSTRATED BY

MELISSA LEE JOHNSON

Routledge
Taylor & Francis Group

NEW YORK AND LONDON

Designed cover image: Illustrated by Melissa Lee Johnson

First published 2023
by Routledge
605 Third Avenue, New York, NY 10158

and by Routledge
4 Park Square, Milton Park, Abingdon, Oxon, OX14 4RN

Routledge is an imprint of the Taylor & Francis Group, an informa business

Illustrated by Melissa Lee Johnson

ISBN: 978-1-032-29347-9 (hbk)
ISBN: 978-1-032-28640-2 (pbk)
ISBN: 978-1-003-30117-2 (ebk)

DOI: 10.4324/9781003301172

Typeset in Futura
by Deanta Global Publishing Services, Chennai, India

Contents

CHAPTER 1

About This Book

DOI: 10.4324/9781003301172-1

The Language Idioms for Inclusivity series is a collection of short, illustrated books for ages 7–14 that use common language idioms/expressions to explore concepts related to inclusivity. This exploration is informed by sociolinguistic and pragmatic research but is written in a readable format, wherein the author poses probing questions to the reader and guides them through linguistic analysis by suggesting possible answers.

This series introduces children to key concepts in linguistics and gives them (and their parents or instructors) a new, language-oriented framework to use when discussing issues of inclusion.

Talk is Out: Discussing Disagreements is the fifth installment in the Language Idioms for Inclusivity series. In this book, the author challenges readers to investigate disagreement as it relates to both language-use and inclusivity. The author does this by (1) explaining the cultural meaning of the idiom, "talk it out"; (2) introducing Facework and Politeness Theory, two frameworks that linguists use to research and understand disagreements; and (3) explaining why the expectation to "talk it out" could make someone feel excluded. The book ends with a description of how understanding the way language works can help us be more inclusive and practical language tips to integrate learning into daily conversations.

As a supplement to traditional curriculum, this book can be used in a Language Arts setting to learn about figurative language; in a Social Studies setting to discuss diversity, equity, inclusion, and belonging; or as an introduction to linguistics, a college-level subject that is not typically offered to K–12 students.

CHAPTER 2

How to Use This Book in Your Teaching Practice

DOI: 10.4324/9781003301172-2

In whichever context you choose to read this book, here are some suggestions for integrating it into teaching.

1. *Always Aloud, Always Together*

When using it in the classroom or at home, read this book aloud with your 7–14-year-old. The concepts in this book are new and abstract, but the tone of the book speaks to a middle-school audience. Likewise, the illustrations are meant to be seen and enhance the intended learning. Experiencing this book together connects the teacher and learner in a way that promotes questioning, critical thinking, and side-by-side learning. These ideas might be just as new for you as they are for your students! What a wonderful opportunity to learn together.

2. *Use Yourself as an Example*

Familiarize yourself with the book before using it in the classroom. After reading through the concepts and examples, try to think of some real language examples from conversations that you've experienced that reflect the intended learning. Be vulnerable and tell your students about a time when you had a terrible disagreement about something important. By using real examples from your real life, you will extend the feeling that this is a mutual learning experience – and an ongoing one! We are never done learning how to communicate with one another. Your students will feel respected and honored that you are placing yourself in the position of "learner" with them.

3. *Reflect in Discussion*

The intended lessons in this book can be practiced and integrated into discussion-based activities. Some ideas:

● On notecards, write examples of topics that people disagree about (ie, "wearing appropriate clothes to school," "teaching evolution," or "pineapples on pizza"). Also on note cards, describe different types of people ("your mom," "a 15-year-old Hispanic boy," etc.). In groups, ask students to pull out one disagreement card and two people cards. Have them discuss whether those two people would agree or disagree about that topic. Why do they think so?

● Using the Practical Language Tips Section at the back of this book, ask students to role play having inclusive conversations. You can use the same topics from the "disagreement cards" above!

4. *Reflect in Writing*

The intended lessons in this series can be practiced and integrated well into writing-based activities. Some ideas:

- Have students create a Belonging Journal. Give weekly writing prompts and allow for 10–15 minutes of writing time for self-reflection. Prompts should offer a range of writing-types, including, but not limited to:

  ○ Brainstorming (list all the topics that you are passionate about and have strong opinions about. Circle the ones that you have had disagreements about with friends or family).

  ○ Self-reflection (write about a time when you had a disagreement with your parent(s). What was it about? Why do you think your parent(s) had different views on that topic than you? When you look back on the disagreement, do you still think you were right? Why or why not?).

  ○ Creative writing (imagine a scene where two people are having a disagreement about school lunch. Now imagine something happens in that scene that causes both people to start laughing. Write a comic strip describing the scene).

- Have students write an editorial essay critiquing this book. Ask them to share their opinion on an idea or topic presented in this book. Do they agree? Do they disagree? What about their cultural and family background influences what they think? Do they think their friends would like the book? Their grandparents? Why or why not?

5. *Reflect in Hypothetical Thinking*

The intended lessons in this book can be practiced and integrated well into hypothetical-thinking activities (which can be realized in writing or in discussion). Some ideas:

- Create a character(s) that has various diverse physical traits. Challenge students to list three controversial opinions that person might have and explain why they think that based on how that person looks. Ask each student to choose whether they would personally agree or disagree with that person.

- Ask students to imagine a hypothetical world (or school) where everyone shares the same opinions about everything, and there are no disagreements. Do they like this world? Is it peaceful? When challenges arise, are people able to solve problems well in this world? Why or why not?

Thank you for choosing this book and engaging with these ideas. For more ideas about or support in using linguistics and inclusivity in the classroom, visit www.mem ralanguageservices.com.

CHAPTER 3

Glossary

DOI: 10.4324/9781003301172-3

attenuators – words, phrases, or sounds that make your statements seem "smaller." For example, phrases like, "a little bit," "a few reasons," and "minor differences"; speaking quietly; and using a low pitch are all linguistic attenuators.

autonomous – when you do things by yourself and are able to make your own choices without needing the approval of others.

cooperative – when you do things with other people and are willing to consider their opinions when you make choices.

cultural scripts – a formula that uses universally understood terms to explain something about your point of view or your culture.

face-threatening act – language strategies that threaten the positive face (the likability/desire to be liked) or negative face (the autonomy/desire not to be bothered) of a person you are talking to.

facework – a range of things that people can do with words to threaten or enhance someone else's reputation during difficult conversations.

hedging particles – a word or phrase that expresses uncertainty, caution, or indecisiveness about the rest of the sentence.

hypothesis – an educated guess that can be tested using the scientific method.

idiomatic expression – a well-known phrase that carries a well-known cultural meaning.

linguists – language scientists; people who study how human language works, both in the brain and out in the world.

negative face – your negative face is the part of you that doesn't want to be bothered by others.

positive face – your positive face is the part of you that wants to be liked by others.

positive politeness strategies – linguistic techniques that help you minimize potential threats to someone's positive face during a disagreement.

provocative – causing annoyance, anger, or another strong emotion on purpose.

reputation – the opinions that are generally held about someone.

verbal – when something is expressed using words.

CHAPTER 4

The Idiom

DOI: 10.4324/9781003301172-4

What does it mean when someone says, "Talk It Out!"?

TALK IT OUT is a phrase you've probably heard your parents or teachers use.

Maybe you heard this phrase when you were having a disagreement with a sibling that was starting to get out of control. Your mom might've said, "you need to go and talk it out together." Or maybe when your class was having a group discussion and half the class had one opinion, while the other half had a different opinion. Your teacher might've said, "ok, let's talk this out."

When someone says, "TALK IT OUT," they are using an **idiomatic expression**. An idiomatic expression is a well-known phrase that carries a well-known cultural meaning. The words in an idiomatic expression don't always make sense if you think about them outside of your cultural context.

For example, when someone says, "We need to *start from scratch*," you know that they mean they *start something over (from the beginning)* – even though the actual words "from scratch" don't mean that on their own. There are lots of idioms in every language and idioms can tell us a lot about the people who speak that language.

In this book we are talking about the idiom, "TALK IT OUT!"

When someone says TALK IT OUT, what they really mean is something like, "have a conversation with your opponent until you understand and accept one another's point of view."

This can be difficult, because understanding and accepting someone else's point of view does not necessarily mean agreeing with it.

Humans disagree with one another a lot. How do we use language to communicate during disagreements? How does language help us to manage interpersonal conflict?

CHAPTER 5

The Linguistic Theory

DOI: 10.4324/9781003301172-5

Language experts, called **linguists**, have thought and argued about this question a lot. Many of them have come up with guesses, also called **hypotheses**, about how language is used during disagreements between people. One well-known way to think about language and disagreement in linguistics is called

Facework

Facework is a range of things that people can do with words to threaten or enhance someone else's reputation during difficult conversations. It can also be thought of as a linguistic strategy to protect your own **reputation**.

You might already be familiar with the idea of needing to "save face." This expression refers to Facework!

Every person has both a **positive face** and a **negative face**. Your positive face is the part of you that wants to be liked by others. Your negative face is the part of you that doesn't want to be bothered by others.

These two faces have opposite desires: your positive face is the part of you that wants to be **cooperative**, while your negative face is the part of you that doesn't.

This makes relationships and interpersonal communication tricky because every person wants to be both cooperative and **autonomous** at the same time … and that's not always possible.

During disagreements, people often use language strategies that threaten the positive face (the likability/desire to be liked) of their opponent. These strategies are a type of **face-threatening act**.

Here are some examples:

- When you **dislike** something about them:

    "Weird sandals, Aman."

- When you **disagree** with them:

    "Why would you wear those shoes to gym class?!"

- When you express **intense emotions** that make them feel unsafe:

    "What the #@%! are those things on your feet?"

- When you have **different values** than they do:

    "I mean, if you want to be the last person to finish the mile, I guess those are the right shoes."

- When you **brag**:

    "My mile time is under seven minutes – bet you can't beat that!"

- When you **interrupt** them:

    "I plan on walking the mi—" "walking the mile is a cop-out!"

- When you bring up **sensitive topics**:

    "Your sandals are giving off some serious Jesus-vibes. Pray for me during the race!"

- When you **misidentify** them:

    "Wait, you're from the desert, right? That explains the shoes."

When we are having a disagreement with someone, we often use direct face-threatening acts on purpose to be **provocative** or mean, like in the example with Aman's sandals. But there are more subtle ways that we threaten the positive face of the people we interact with. Face-threatening acts aren't always mean, and they are not always **verbal**.

Apologizing, complementing, crying, being embarrassed, or telling a secret all threaten the positive face of the speaker.

- Your positive face is threatened when you are caught writing the answer to a quiz question on your hand.

- Your mom's positive face is threatened when you roll your eyes at her in front of your friends after she asks you to wash your hands before eating from the bag of chips.

- Kareem's positive face is threatened when you say, "I like your new haircut."

- Shay's positive face is threatened when you say, "I'm sorry, this spot is taken."

Even though threatening someone's positive face can look and sound a lot of different ways, it always involves drawing unwanted attention to the other person, or calling them out.

The impact of threatening someone's positive face is that you make them feel isolated – and excluded – either intentionally or unintentionally.

Face-threatening acts and the feeling of exclusion that they cause is what makes us feel bad when we argue. This is why we don't want to TALK IT OUT with our opponents – it's much easier to disagree without having to confront someone so that we can avoid all of the threats to our positive face.

But we know that if we don't talk to one another, we will never understand our opponent's point of view. Is there a way to disagree with someone while avoiding threats to our positive face?

Is there a way to disagree with someone while avoiding threats to our positive face?

CHAPTER 6

The Inclusive Solution

DOI: 10.4324/9781003301172-6

Thankfully, Facework Theory also tells us how to minimize potential threats to positive face during a disagreement. Here are four techniques Linguists call **Positive Politeness Strategies**.

1. *Share things you like about your opponent*

    a. **I'm so glad you're taking this issue so seriously**, *but I don't agree with the conclusion you've drawn.*

2. *Re-state your opponent's argument so that they know you heard them*

    a. **So your position is that** *individual clothing choices highlight differences and distract students. And your solution to this problem is school uniforms. Am I understanding you correctly?*

3. *Make the problem seem manageable (use **attenuators**)*

    a. *It is true that differences can be distracting. But I think where we disagree **a little bit** is in your suggestion that these differences – even when they distract us – are bad.*

4. *Soften direct language (use **hedging particles**)*

    a. **Maybe we could** *come up with a solution that would teach students to notice differences and accept them without being distracted. **I'm not sure** removing those differences all together will help do that.*

You can't control the kind of language that your opponent might use, but by choosing to avoid threatening their positive face, you set the tone for the argument and encourage them to follow.

Humans disagree with one another a lot. And when we choose to TALK IT OUT, the language we use to communicate during disagreements often threatens one another's positive face and makes each person feel excluded.

Understanding how Facework works, and learning positive politeness strategies to avoid face-threatening acts, can help us manage interpersonal conflict.

Linguistics helps us TALK IT OUT in a way that is productive, moving past differences and into acceptance and understanding.

CHAPTER 7

Practical Language Tips

DOI: 10.4324/9781003301172-7

The Positive Politeness Strategies outlined in this book can be a good place to start to be more inclusive during disagreements.

Sometimes, though, when you are disagreeing with someone whose cultural background is completely different from your own, the politeness strategies are not enough.

For example, one strategy is to "soften direct language" (instead of saying, "Close the window," choosing to say, "I'm a little chilly in here! Would you mind closing the window?"). Softening direct language works well for many cultures, but some cultures in the world value direct language so highly that softening it might make the disagreement worse, not better!

These kinds of cross-cultural disagreements can be especially challenging, but linguists have come up with a strategy for those as well.

Using **Cultural Scripts** to Explain Your Position.

A cultural script is a formula that uses **universally understood terms** to explain something about your point of view or your culture.

Here is a list of some of the universally understood terms:

- Good

- Bad

- Say

- Think

- Want

- People

- If

- because

Here is the formula (script) for using these terms:

1. TOPIC: *(the idea you are talking about)*.

2. WHO: *(your cultural group)* **thinks** *like this*.

3. CIRCUMSTANCE: *when I* **(want, say, or think) something**.

4. POSITIVE OUTCOME: *it is **good if people think*** ...

5. NEGATIVE OUTCOME: *it is **bad if people think*** ...

This script uses only terms that are universally understood to explain in a very clear and simple way why someone thinks a certain way, or shares the same cultural value.

Here is an example of how you might use a cultural script to explain (using ONLY universally understood terms) your position on pronouns.

1. TOPIC: *gender.*

2. WHO: *Americans born after 2000 think like this.*

3. CIRCUMSTANCE: *when talking about others whose gender identity has not been shared.*

4. POSITIVE OUTCOME: *it is good to say "they."*

5. NEGATIVE OUTCOME: *it is not good to say "he" or "she."*

This might seem too simplistic to you, especially if you are passionate about the topic and would like to say more. But if your goal is mutual understanding, limiting your explanation to the universally understood terms is the best way to prevent confusion.

Cultural Scripts should not be used to tell someone that their culture is bad. Rather, they should be used to explain how your culture thinks about something in a way that uses cross-cultural universals. This is a great way to begin a discussion that will likely contain a disagreement, because it is a kind way to make sure that everyone understands what is being discussed.

Bibliography

Bibliography

Ahearn, L. M. (2021). *Living language: An introduction to linguistic anthropology*. John Wiley & Sons.

Archer, D. (2015). Slurs, insults,(backhanded) compliments and other strategic facework moves. *Language Sciences, 52*, 82–97.

Archer, D., Aijmer, K., & Wichmann, A. (2013). *Pragmatics: An advanced resource book for students*. Routledge.

Brown, P., Levinson, S. C., & Levinson, S. C. (1987). *Politeness: Some universals in language usage* (Vol. 4). Cambridge University Press.

Goddard, C., & Wierzbicka, A. (2004). Cultural scripts: What are they and what are they good for? *Intercultural Pragmatics, 1–2*, 153–166.

Tollison, A. C. (2005). Extending the politeness theory to meditation discourse: Does facework make a difference? Masters's Thesis, University of Tenessee. https://trace.tennessee.edu/utk_gradthes/4594/

Meet the Author and Illustrator

Meet the Author

Samantha Beaver is a linguist. She got her Master's Degree in Applied English Linguistics from the University of Wisconsin-Madison. Sociolinguistics, Pragmatics, and Conversation Analysis are her areas of linguistic expertise, and her favorite topics to explore are language equity, language and gender, language learning, language and people management, and language and power. When she's not doing linguistic work for other people, she is at home fostering the language development of her two sons, Simon and Louis. You can learn more about Samantha's work at www.memrala nguageservices.com.

Meet the Illustrator

Melissa Lee Johnson is an award-winning artist, illustrator, and graphic designer. She graduated with a Bachelor of Fine Arts in Integrated Studio Arts from the Milwaukee Institute of Art and Design and got her start illustrating for an alternative newspaper. In 2020 she received the Communication Arts Illustration Annual Award of Excellence in Advertising. She currently works for Made By Things, a small animation studio based in Columbus, Ohio. When she's not drawing, she likes to hang with Bambi, Sparkle, and Trixie, her three rescue Chihuahuas. You can learn more about her at melissaleejohnsonart.com.

Samantha and Melissa became best friends when they were middle schoolers. Even back then, they often imagined teaming up to write and illustrate a book together someday. The content of this book is especially meaningful for them, because it wasn't always easy to remain friends and accept each other's differences and decisions as they grew into adults. A patient persistence has allowed them to hold fast to what now feels like sisterhood, and they hope that readers of this book learn that the best way to love someone who is different from you is to simply *keep trying*.